A TURN FOR THE VERSE

LIMERICKS WITH A TWIST

A TURN FOR THE VERSE

LIMERICKS WITH A TWIST

LEWIS M. GEDIMAN

ILLUSTRATIONS BY
ROBERT SEAMAN

MUSE INK PRESS

Published by Muse Ink Press
1465 East Putnam Avenue, Suite 529
Old Greenwich, CT06870

First Edition

Printed in the United States of American

ISBN 978-0-9859915-6-2

For Sarah and Elizabeth

CONTENTS

FOREWORD

Limericks go back several centuries at least—well before Edward Lear, who, though he employed the form, did not use the word, which can be traced much further back, and which, yes, probably did have a connection to the city of Limerick in Ireland.

The limerick form has been tweaked and twisted in various ways over the years. For a time, early on, the last line was a reprise of the first. Ludicrous situations or persons have often been a theme. Wordplay of different types, including pure nonsense, has come and gone and come again. Throughout, two basic characteristics have held sway: (1) Limericks are not serious; they may be satiric, parodic, or lexically contrived, but their intent is humorous. (2) Over much of their history, many if not most limericks have been "dirty" —ranging from the simply scatological, through various subjects and degrees of naughty or bawdy, to the more sophisticated and inventively obscene.

It's on this second pillar that, to a great extent, I depart from tradition. True, in order to retain at least some formal cred, I have felt obliged to include a few specimens of questionable taste, but by and large this collection—however puerile, solopsistic, or otherwise offensive it may be—is pretty damn clean (for limericks). To drive home this point, and with a nod to one of the most famous limericks of all:

> That infamous man from Nantucket
> Discovered a hole in his bucket.
> Believe it or not,
> That's all that I've got
> About that young man from Nantucket.

As with most other forms of wordplay, many people have tried their hand at limericks, and given the rather narrow focus, it's possible, even likely, that some of the narrative notions and rhymes included here have been put forth by others. Not having made an exhaustive study of the literature, I cannot guarantee 100 percent originality. But I can assert that to the best of my conscious knowledge, and for better or worse, this collection is entirely my (ir)responsibility.

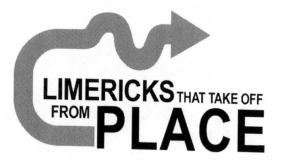

LIMERICKS THAT TAKE OFF FROM PLACE

A housekeeper up in Vancouver
Tried vacuuming each window louver.
Though awkward to do,
She vacuumed a few,
Then decided it didn't beHoover.

A Cambridge professor named Lunt
Took pleasure in giving affront:
In his boat he would ram
Other craft on the Cam;
And when he was challenged, he'd punt.

A pretty young girl from Murmansk
Was keen on a trip to Gdansk.
She got quite upset
When her parents said Nyet!—
And looked at her rather askansk.

A student in Wilmington, Del.
Did not know orthography well.
Once during a drill
He felt dizzy and ill
And asked, "May I sit for a spell?"

British cuisine is unique,
In texture and taste rather bleak.
Their bangers and mash
Should go straight to the trash,
And likewise their bubble-and-squeak.

A fellow from Little Rock, Ark.
Joined a bird-watching group in the park.
With interest not strong
He didn't stay long,
Since he just tried it out for a lark.

All girls at the dress works in Chester
Have compound first names (except Hester).
There's Anna-Marie,
Sarah-Jane, Betsy-Lee,
Nancy-Jo and, of course, Polly-Esther.

In Outer Mongolia, Bert
Dined with his wife in their yurt.
The main course was yak
In a double-ribbed rack.
God knows what they had for dessert!

I suppose you could look upon Iceland,
Though cold, as a modestly nice land.
For food, one might wish
For a little less fish,
And it's no use at all as a rice land.

Few people in Saginaw, Mich.
Have seen, much less tasted, a knish.
But if they should spy one
And venture to try one,
I'll bet they would find it delish!

Los Angeles weatherman Lawrence
Remarked to his lady friend Florence,
"I see in South Bay
Bad weather holds sway—
Indeed, it is raining in Torrance."

An Eskimo ancient named Joe
Was dying—and ready to go.
Supporting his mission
In native tradition,
His kin said, "Let's go with the floe."

We all know that German beer's swell.
The braumeisters ply their craft well.
Their dark beer and light
Afford equal delight,
So I can chug dunkel* like hell**.

Adventurous seafaring Irma,
Returning to home *terra firma*,
Told tales; not the least
Were about the Far East—
Although she called Myanmar Burma.

*In German, dark-colored beer.
**In German, light-colored beer.

JoAnn from Peoria, Ill.
Of factory work had her fill.
So clearly worn down,
When the plant quit the town
She looked like she'd been through the mill.

I recently wondered anew
If Dutch footwear rumor is true.
I've heard much about it
But still tend to doubt it—
As most people would, wooden shoe?

In Greater New York and surround,
Where water and accents abound,
What I truly hold dear
Is to see and to hear
That ubiquitous Lawn Guyland Sound.

Farsi's a learning excursion,
Best done via total immersion.
A book or CD
Wouldn't do it for me—
I'd rather work Persian to Persian.

I know of a woman named Monica
Who lives by the shore in Salonika.
She says, "Yes, it's true
There is not much to do—
I go fishing and play the harmonica."

O'Leary's saloon in Del Mar
Was aging and way below par.
Its standards so low
The town council could show
That O'Leary had best raze the bar.

An Israeli young woman named Nora
Was transferred to far Bora Bora.
At big celebrations
Her dancing gyrations
Became much more hula than hora.

In Saudi Arabia, Jake
Had a stripper jump out of a cake.
For all of the while
Awaiting his trial
He prayed that he'd get a fair sheik.

A saucy young flirt from Van Nuys
Was constantly teasing the guys.
In particular, she
Was tickled to see
Their attention *et al.* on the rise.

In suburban Chicago, young Brett
Was looking for lodgings to let
When he happened to meet
A nice chap on the street
Who cried out, "Hail, fellow, Wilmette!"

I knew a detective named Stu
Whose successful detections were few.
He didn't lack heart,
But he wasn't that smart,
And in most cases hadn't a clue.

A farmer named Roger McGraw
Had no great respect for the law.
When he stole, one fine day,
His neighbor's new hay,
The judge said, "Now, that's the last straw!"

Being a poet's a curse;
For money and fame, nothing's worse.
And yet we persist
As if we'd be missed
If our rhyming should cease. How per-verse!

A shortage of dough was indeed
Very hard for a baker named Reed.
He said, "You can bet
That I knead what I get,
But I don't always get what I need."

A spirited dancer named Pete
Thought he'd tap-dance his way down the
    street.
Ignoring the cusses
Of cars, trucks, and buses,
He tapped to the end—what a feat!

Cole Porter's songs gave a thrill
To a moonshine producer named Bill.
His special delight
Was "The Still of the Night"—
But he called it "The Night of the Still."

An Amsterdam jeweler named Stroop
Sought to join a professional group.
It came as a blow
When the guild voted no,
Thus leaving Stroop out of the loupe.

Invited to share a nice smoke,
The chef thought he'd try a small joke.
He said, "Yes, indeed,
Since I'm partial to weed,
I'll gladly indulge in a toque."

Sister Margaret Mary Ignatius
Confiscated a skin mag salacious.
She stole a quick peek,
Gave a gasp and a squeak:
"Oh, dear Lord!
"Mercy me!
"Goodness gracious!"

Chef Mahmoud was known to be quirky,
His restaurant's ethos quite murky.
But one time, at least,
For the Thanksgiving feast,
He turned to the East and talked Turkey.

A flutist who played on the street
Kept watch for the cop on the beat.
For if he would see him,
He needed to flee him
And find a new venue *toot sweet.*

Short-order cook Tommy Brown
Made breakfasts of local renown.
His eggs, ham, and grits
Were dependable hits,
And they came with the toast of the town.

A strict, by-the-book county judge
Was mostly unwilling to budge.
His weakness was treats,
In particular, sweets,
Which sometimes could lead him to fudge.

Officer Oliver Finch
Was known to be mean as The Grinch.
But peers will attest
That when on an arrest
There's no better cop in a pinch.

A sugar beet grower named Blaine
Lost much of his crop due to rain.
He said, "I was wrong
To have waited so long—
Next season I think I'll raise cane."

In stories of shoemaking past,
Some cobblers were known to be fast.
When Tony would race,
At least he would place,
And sometimes was first from the last.

Speaking of people who bake,
There's pastry chef Christopher Blake.
His fruit tarts and scones
Spark erogenous zones,
But his Boston Cream Pie takes the cake.

Roger The Researcher's data
Turned out to be filled with errata.
Professional peers
Soon retracted their cheers
And declared him *persona non grata*.

Experienced carpenter Neville
Was practiced at mortise and bevel.
In piercing a wall
He would give it his awl,
But his billing was not on the level.

A novice attorney named Mort
Botched a small civil action in court.
"Just wasn't my day,"
He said with dismay.
"Try again," was the judge's re-tort.

A trip to the dentist for Jill
Was a harrowing prospect until
She got in the chair
And said to him there,
"Go ahead, Doc, we both know the drill."

At the actors' hotel in Bordeaux
It was cold and had started to snow.
When the old furnace broke
And the residents woke,
The cry rang out, "On with the chaud!"

In his garden, a parson one day
Found that beetles were having their way.
His wife saw them too
And cried, "What should we do?"
The parson intoned, "Let us spray."

Dog breeder Benjamin Clark
Had a Rottweiler fierce as a shark.
Folks who came near
Were advised to stay clear,
For his bite was far worse than his bark.

A seamstress who lived in South Bend
Fell ill and was fearing the end.
But then she came 'round,
Grew increasingly sound,
And soon she was back on the mend.

LIMERICKS ABOUT
MISHAPS,
MISFORTUNES
& MAYHEM

An anarchist living on Guam
Decided to build his own bomb.
But he wasn't precise
On the timing device. . .
Let us now say the 23rd Psalm.

There once was a woman named Stella
Who couldn't stop eating Nutella.
She met a sad fate
When she gained so much weight
That Guido, her beau, said "Ciao, bella!"

A clumsy old geezer named Lutz
Inadvertently sat on his nuts.
In spite of the pain
He did it again,
And again and again—what a klutz!

So taken with Twitter was Pete
That even when crossing the street
He couldn't postpone
A quick check of his phone. . .
And was struck by a truck in mid-tweet.

An infant in Hattiesburg, Miss.
Was, unbeknownst, brought to his bris.
'Mid relatives' cheers
He thought through his tears,
"I do believe something's amiss!"

Ever adventurous, Bradley
Agreed to go sky-diving (gladly).
It pains me to tell
That it didn't go well
When his 'chute failed to operate (sadly).

Though born to the throne, poor Queen Jane
Considered the title a pain.
One day in a torrent,
She cried, "It's abhorrent!
I'm coming in out of the reign."

Aspiring chorus girl Roxy
Was kept as a hedge funder's doxy.
Her stage debut failed,
Her boyfriend was jailed.
She's gone back in tears to Biloxi.

Jack Moore of Iowa City
Was called on to rescue a kitty.
He climbed up the tree,
Got the animal free,
But then slipped and fell—Moore's the pity.

Last fall Mary Ellen and Bing
Were engaged in an amorous fling.
But just at the start
The old bed fell apart,
So they had to resume in the spring.

As some of our faculties wane,
We older folks tend to complain.
We speak with regret
Of how much we forget
When we wander down Memory Lane.

A Dublin philanderer reckless
Atoned to his wife with a necklace.
She flung it aside
And angrily cried,
"Now there's *two* ways you'll be feckless!"

At the Asian food festival, Murray
Ran off to the john in a hurry.
He returned pale and weak,
But he managed to speak:
"It's not the pla goong, it's the curry."

Always a risk-taker, Dwight
Had his heart set on unaided flight.
He leaped out to soar
From the twenty-third floor,
But did he stay airborne? Not quite.

In hopes of some test satisfaction,
The engineer sprang into action.
But the gear-gripper failed
That he thought he had nailed,
Thus driving the chap to dystraction.

Drunk and disorderly Carter
Reached out for a pole dancer's garter.
She twisted away
And then swung 'round to say,
"That's definitely a non-starter!"

A fellow from Fond du Lac, Wisc.
Was rather addicted to risk.
He walked on thin ice
And fell through it twice.
He should have known better—tsk! tsk!

Increasingly desperate, Flo
Was seeking a suitable beau.
Three first-dates went badly,
Reminding her, sadly,
Of Curley and Larry and Moe.

The letter began "Mon Cher Jean*
By the time you read this I'll be gone."
Though filled with despair,
Did he feel lurking there
Some relief? Well, perhaps a *soupçon*.

*French pronunciation: *Zshon.*

My memory problems are chronic,
With places and names it's ironic:
I've tried all the tricks
To ensure a thing sticks,
But then I forget the mnemonic!

A student of English named Steve
Said, "Mastery's hard to achieve:
The spelling's abusive;
And meaning's elusive
In words such as 'sanction' and 'cleave'."

General George Armstrong Custer
Led all of the troops he could muster
To Little Bighorn,
Whereupon he was shorn
Of pretty much all of his luster.

When grandmother cooked, you could bet it
Would not do her heritage credit.
In tasting her tsimmis
A **statue** would grimace—
And as for her latkes, forget it!

In need, on a flight supersonic,
Of a gastrointestinal tonic,
And a bit overwrought,
The poor chap had this thought:
"What a place for a good high colonic!"

A dog and a cat in Seattle
Would now and then fall into battle.
Their owner (named Dave)
Said, "The dog can behave,
But I very much doubt if the cat'll.

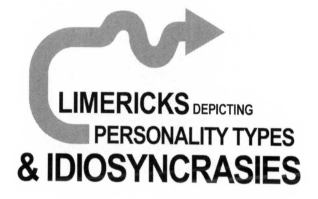

LIMERICKS DEPICTING PERSONALITY TYPES & IDIOSYNCRASIES

An odd chap from upstate New York
Enjoyed eating soup with a fork.
Asked why, he would say,
"It lasts longer that way,
And I dearly love soup." What a dork!

A temptress, the Princess Louise,
Brought strong men to tears, on their knees.
With smouldering glances
She'd hint at romances,
And then have them hanged—what a tease!

A chef from Jamaica named Kirk
Grew very extreme in his work:
His chicken with spices
Would give rise to crisis,
And diners would cry, "What a jerk!"

A clerk, in a moment of pique,
Mooned a dowager in a boutique.
Though rather astonished,
She promptly admonished
The rascal, exclaiming "What cheek!"

A man with a high-minded credo
Of keeping streets safe in Toledo
Spent much of his time
Fighting bad guys and crime,
Wearing only a cape and a Speedo.

An ill-tempered fellow named Springer
Was often inclined to malinger.
He'd well understand
When folks asked for a hand,
But instead he would give them the finger.

A crude lout from Peabody, Mass.
Was tutored to make him less crass.
When asked to assess
If he'd had much success,
He replied, "Did it help? Bet your ass!"

A menacing black-suited ninja
Would leap, kick, and twist to unhinja.
But all just in play,
For he'd smile and then say,
"You thought you were in for it, dinja?"

A talented techie named Zeke
Was steeped in computer mystique.
To call him a nerd
Isn't quite the right word,
But you surely could call him a geek.

A strange girl I knew, name of Molly,
Found transport by streetcar quite jolly.
She rode them all day,
Causing people to say
She's as on as she's off of her trolley.

Joe-Billy liked hamhocks and grits,
But nearly all fruits gave him fits.
Plums, peaches, and berries,
And most of all, cherries,
Would make him exclaim, "It's the pits!"

A fast-talking fence we'll call Chuck
Liked to cite his exceptional luck.
Asked often enough
Where he got all his stuff,
He'd reply, "It just fell off the truck!"

A grumpy old barfly named Stone
Had run out of cash on his own.
When a guy that he knew
Said he'd spring for a few,
Stone muttered "Just leave me a loan."

A vain couple, Todd and Monique,
Were in thrall to the fashion mystique.
On the *haute couture* scene
The pair was quite keen
To be seen as they danced chic to chic.

Pastries and hookers, for Bart,
Were two things most dear to his heart.
When pressed to aver
Which delight he'd prefer,
He smiled and said, "I'll take the tart."

Pursuing life's manifold trails,
Young Jack was no stranger to jails.
Not only was Jack
Often on the wrong track—
He sometimes ran clear off the rails.

A new-agey stoner named Scott
Liked to smoke marijuana a lot.
For his job, with a grin,
He said "Phoning it in
Is how I keep going to pot."

One-legged Senator Trump
Was known as a bit of a grump.
But come the election
He gained some affection
With speeches he made on the stump.

Dead set against neckwear was Clyde;
He went open-collared with pride.
He once got a call
To a fancy dress ball—
Poor fellow was fit to be tied.

My granny's clairvoyance was fine;
The Internet she did divine
When back in the day
She conjured a way
Of drying her laundry online.

No fellow was stronger or sweeter
Than six-foot-six "Man Mountain" Peter.
At popular pubs
And the trendiest clubs,
He could serve as both bouncer and greeter.

I knew a strange fellow named Kent
Who slept doubled up in a tent.
When he asked if I thought
That a chap hadn't ought,
I said, "Fine, if it's truly your bent."

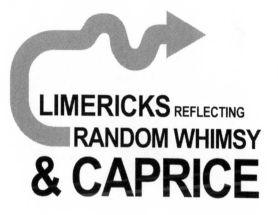

LIMERICKS REFLECTING
RANDOM WHIMSY
& CAPRICE

As everyone surely agrees:
If you work on the flying trapeze,
A blink or a cough
Might not put your act off—
But there'll be hell to pay if you sneeze.

Ever since I was a kid
I would now and then slip off the grid.
And even though Freud
Might be rather annoyed,
I would swap superego for id.

Though William was catnip to Jill,
It looked like her chances were nil.
Withal, she kept trying
And brooked no denying
That when there's a way, there's a Will.

A spider from Omaha, Neb.
Was keen to become a celeb.
In film and TV
It was not meant to be,
But his name came to fame on the Web.

Here's Lola, quite pleasingly rounded
And ready for frolics unbounded.
Her joints are elastic
Her tricks quite fantastic.
She'll leave you done in but astounded.

A man got his odd name of Joyce
At his birth, so it wasn't his choice.
When he later arranged
To have his name changed,
He was happy, but didn't re-Joyce.

I asked an agnostic named Steven
What deity he might believe in:
"Would you go for the odds
On malevolent gods?"
"No," he responded, "not even."

The Critique of Pure Reason by Kant
Lends a dense philosophical slant.
We know that indeed
It's quite daunting to read.
We probably should—but we shan't.

Attila (no friend of a comb)
Went plundering halfway to Rome,
While Mrs. Attila
(Who loved that gorilla)
Kept waiting for "Hunny, I'm home!"

Banks are all over the place,
Each brand with its corporate face.
With not many clues
As to which one to choose,
You might as well cut to the Chase.

How awful for Little Bo Peep,
That time she lost track of her sheep.
But she needn't have feared,
For they soon reappeared.
Astonished, she cried, "What the...(bleep)!!"

Here's something I marvel at still:
How whales get to feed to their fill.
They sweep through the seas
With the greatest of ease,
All the while moving in for the krill.

Origami's not easy, I'm told,
With creases both subtle and bold.
It takes patience and care
And finesse brought to bear
By anyone new to the fold.

Lady Godiva, of course,
Rode nude into town on her horse.
She did it at night,
So the scandal was slight—
In daytime it would have been worse.

In a quiz where I needed to choose
Among history's dwarfs who made news,
It wasn't by chance
That my thoughts turned to France,
Where of course I had little Toulouse.

The iPhone she constantly taps
Is Sally's religion, perhaps.
Always in search
Even when she's in church,
Where she takes special joy in the apse.

ACKNOWLEDGEMENTS

I am reliably informed that it is no great privilege to be in bed with someone who, in the wee hours, is likely to sit bolt upright, nudge you with an elbow, and announce, "I think I've got one!"—this followed by a halting recitation of yet another new limerick for which the world is presumably not yearning. Accordingly, I want to thank my loving and steadfast wife Judy, whose fervent wish for me to either get over it or make a book of it I choose to regard as encouragement and support, and whose editorial acumen and reader's sensibility have been invaluable.

In addition, I want to thank my publisher, Joanne Dearcopp of Muse Ink Press, for her general guidance, unerring judgment, and technical expertise—to say nothing of her keen insight, relentless patience and good cheer—that helped bring this project to life.

ABOUT THE AUTHOR

A repeat offender in language abuse, Lewis M. Gediman earlier published *Semantricks: A Dictionary of Words You Thought You Knew.* Not content with the linguistic mayhem perpetrated in simple prose there, he turns his hand to verse with this new work, inflicting a variety of twists and turns on the familiar and well-loved (by some) limerick form. In a former incarnation, he was president of a marketing research and consulting firm, in which capacity he conducted countless interviews and focus groups on subjects ranging from dog food to remote-control-handling devices for nuclear hot labs. These days he can be found in Stamford, Connecticut, where he lives with his wife and no cats.

ABOUT THE ILLUSTRATOR

Robert Seaman is an illustrator, fine artist, teacher and occasional cartoonist. His illustrations appear in Hoagy Carmichael's two volume *History of the Grand Cascapedia River* and three other books by the same author. Over the years his work has appeared in Massachusetts Audubon's *Sanctuary Magazine*, *Fly Fisherman Magazine*, *Ladybug* and *Cricket* magazines, and is being used by a number of greeting card and other publishers. His "fine art" work may be seen on the web site www.368ART.com, which he shares with his designer daughter.

ALSO BY THE AUTHOR

Semantricks: A Dictionary of Words
You Thought You Knew
(Thomas Dunne Books/St. Martin's Griffin; 2008)

. . . is the result of associative thinking run amok combined with the impulse control of a fruit fly. Many of the definitions are simple puns (e.g., *Paradigms: 20 cents . . . Brussels: business side of Belgian hairbrush*). But there's also a more sophisticated variant wherein the definition also contains a reference to the meaning of the given word (e.g., *Tarantula: deadly Italian folk dance. . . Gravel: humble oneself in the driveway*). Beyond that, some of the entries comprise multiple-word riffs, with phonetic or conceptual links providing the literary pleasure equivalent of a compound fracture:

Pillage:	theft of medication
Spillage:	clumsy pillage
Rubbery:	massage parlor
Rubbish:	inferior rubbery service
Sham:	imitation ham
Spam:	real sham
Scam:	imitation Spam

Semantricks revels (wallows, actually) in aural and ideational associations that will surprise, amuse, challenge and occasionally scandalize the word-savvy reader. It is available via Amazon (including a Kindle edition), where, believe it or not, favorable reader reviews can be found.

89218836R00064

Made in the USA
Lexington, KY
24 May 2018